EUROPEAN COUNTRIES TODAY

FRANCE

EUROPEAN COUNTRIES TODAY

TITLES IN THE SERIES

EUROPEAN COUNTRIES TODAY
FRANCE

Dominic J. Ainsley

MASON CREST

Mason Crest
450 Parkway Drive, Suite D
Broomall, Pennsylvania PA 19008
(866) MCP-BOOK (toll free)

First printing
9 8 7 6 5 4 3 2 1

ISBN: 978-1-4222-3983-4
Series ISBN: 978-1-4222-3977-3
ebook ISBN: 978-1-4222-7798-0

Printed in the United States of America

Library of Congress Cataloging-in-Publication Data

Names: Ainsley, Dominic J., author.
Title: France / Dominic J. Ainsle.
Description: Broomall, Pennsylvania : Mason Crest, 2019. | Series: European
  countries today | Includes index.
Identifiers: LCCN 2018007575 (print) | LCCN 2018018415 (ebook) | ISBN
  9781422277980 (eBook) | ISBN 9781422239834 (hardback)
Subjects: LCSH: France--Juvenile literature.
Classification: LCC DC17 (ebook) | LCC DC17 .A56 2019 (print) | DDC 944--dc23 LC record available at
https://lccn.loc.gov/2018007575

Cover images
Main: *Abbey of Sénanque, Provence.*
Left: *French wine.*
Center: *Eiffel Tower.*
Right: *Couple in a Parisian café.*

QR CODES AND LINKS TO THIRD-PARTY CONTENT

CONTENTS

KEY ICONS TO LOOK FOR:

Words to Understand: These words with their easy-to-understand definitions will increase the reader's understanding of the text while building vocabulary skills.

Sidebars: This boxed material within the main text allows readers to build knowledge, gain insights, explore possibilities, and broaden their perspectives by weaving together additional information to provide realistic and holistic perspectives.

Educational Videos: Readers can view videos by scanning our QR codes, providing them with additional content to supplement the text. Examples include news coverage, moments in history, speeches, iconic sports moments, and much more!

Text-Dependent Questions: These questions send the reader back to the text for more careful attention to the evidence presented there.

Research Projects: Readers are pointed toward areas of further inquiry connected to each chapter. Suggestions are provided for projects that encourage deeper research and analysis.

FRANCE AT A GLANCE

MAP OF EUROPE

RUSSIA

GEORGIA

AZEI

ARMENIA

The Geography of France

Location: Western Europe, bordering the Bay of
  Biscay and the English Channel, between
  Belgium and Spain; bordering the
  Mediterranean Sea between Italy and Spain.

Area: slightly smaller than twice the size of
  Colorado
  total: 211,210 square miles (547,030 sq. km)
  land: 210,669 square miles (545,630 sq. km)
  water: 541 square miles (1,400 sq. km)

Borders: Andorra 35 miles (57 km), Belgium 385
  miles (620 km), Germany 280 miles (451
  km), Italy 303 miles (488 km), Luxembourg
  45 miles (73 km), Monaco 3 miles (4 km),
  Spain 387 miles (623 km), Switzerland 356
  miles (573 km)

Climate: cool winters and mild summers, but mild
  winters and hot summers along the
  Mediterranean; occasional strong, cold, dry,
  north to northwesterly wind known as mistral

Terrain: mostly flat plains or gently rolling hills in
  the north and west; mountainous elsewhere,
  Pyrenees in the south and the Alps in the east

Elevation extremes:
  lowest point: Rhone River delta -7 feet (-2
  meters) highest point: Mont Blanc 15,771 feet
  (4,807 meters)

  Natural hazards: flooding, avalanches,
    midwinter windstorms, drought, forest
    fires in the south

Source: www.cia.gov 2017

Flag of France

After the Ukraine and Russia, France is the third largest country in Europe. It is composed of a wide variety of landscapes, including four upland areas: the Alps, the Pyrenees, the Massifs of Brittany and the Central Plateau. The large lowland areas are drained by rivers such as the Garonne, Rhône, Loire, and Seine. France has had a long history: the earliest conquerors were the Romans in 50 BEC. and the latest were the Germans who invaded in both World Wars, although Germany is now one of France's closest allies. The flag dates back to the Revolution of 1789 and is one of the most recognizable in the world. Called the tricolore, it is said to represent liberty, equality, fraternity, signifying the Republican ideal.

ABOVE: *Parisian cafés, such as this one, have always been popular with painters, writers, and philosophers, including great artists such as Pablo Picasso, Georges Bataille, and Robert Desnos.*

The People of France

Population: 64,836,154

Ethnic groups: Celtic and Latin with Teutonic, Slavic, North
    African, Indochinese and Basque minorities

Age structure:
    0–14 years: 18.59%
    15–64 years: 62.29%
    65 years and over: 19.12%

Population growth rate: 0.41%

Birth rate: 12.3 births/1,000 pop.

Death rate: 9.3 deaths/1,000 pop.

Migration rate: 1.1 migrant(s)/1,000 pop.

Infant mortality rate: 3.3 deaths/1,000 live births

Life expectancy at birth:
    Total population: 81.8 years
    Male: 78.7 years
    Female: 85.1 years

Total fertility rate: 2.07 children born/woman

Religions: Christian (mainly Roman Catholic) 63–66%,
Jewish 0.5–0.75%, Buddhist 0.5–0.75%, Muslim 7–9%,
unaffiliated 0.5–1.0%, none 23–28%

Languages: French

Literacy rate: 99%

Source: www.cia.gov 2017

9

Words to Understand

lichens: A type of small hardy plants that grows on rocks and walls.

navigable: A waterway deep and wide enough to afford passage to ships.

timberline: The upper limit of tree growth in mountains or high latitudes.

BELOW: Tende is a small town perched on the side a hill in the Alpes-Maritimes department of southeast Provence. It lies about 50 miles (80 km) inland from the French Riviera and in the mountains close to the border with Italy. Interestingly, it was only in 1947 that the town passed from Italy to France.

Chapter One
FRANCE'S GEOGRAPHY & LANDSCAPE

*B*ienvenue à France! In other words, welcome to France. The largest country in Western Europe, France is a place where the old and the new exist together; ancient Roman ruins can be seen right next to modern-day houses, and medieval towns are just minutes away from bustling urban centers. Breathtakingly beautiful, France is a popular tourist destination, and has been for centuries.

Geography

France's geography is incredibly varied. The south and central regions are hills, while plains and lowlands form the northern area. Then there are the Alps to the east and the Pyrenees to the south. These huge mountains form equally

ABOVE: *Mont Blanc in the Alps is reflected in the Lacs des Chéserys, near Chamonix.*

Educational Video

This 16-minute video provides a brief insight into France's geography. Scan the QR code with your phone to watch!

impressive valleys filled with all kinds of plant and animal life. The Alps are a natural boundary passable only by taking narrow zigzagging roads up and down the mountains. Driving on these almost too-narrow roads, a tourist may marvel as the natives zoom up and down at impressive speed, seeming to show no concern for the fact that the car is hundreds of feet in the air and that there is no guardrail, or even shoulder, protecting the unwary from falling to the valley below.

ABOVE: *Eurostar is a passenger train service between London and continental Europe that passes through the Channel Tunnel.*

France's Neighbors

Around twice the size of Colorado, France has an area of 211,210 square miles (547,030 square kilometers). While the country is bordered to the west, northwest, and southeast by water, France has many neighboring countries as well. These include Belgium, Luxembourg, Germany, Switzerland, Monaco, and Italy to the north and east, as well as Spain and Andorra to the south.

It is a short distance across the English Channel (La Manche, or "the Sleeve," in French) to England, and many tourists travel the Channel Tunnel (the tunnel that spans the English Channel) in both directions. With so many English tourists visiting France regularly, it is not uncommon to see a car with the driver on the right-hand side, even in the southernmost parts of the country.

ABOVE: The makeshift refugee camp called the "Jungle" in Calais, where migrants stayed before attempting to cross the English Channel. The camp was closed in 2016.

ABOVE: The Lighthouse of Brittany. Brittany is in the northwest of France next to the Atlantic Ocean and consequently has a very changeable climate. Warm sunshine often gives way to strong winds and storms.

The Climate

Because of the wind that blows off the Atlantic Ocean, bringing warm temperatures with it, France has a relatively moderate climate. This results in mild winters and cool summers, with temperatures in the French capital of Paris rarely getting below 34° to 40°F (1° to 6°C) in the winter or above 55° to 75°F (13° to 24°C) in the summer. While this proximity to the sea means a warmer climate, the winds that travel through France also bring precipitation. Because of this, it is not uncommon for skies to be overcast and for a steady drizzle to fall from the clouds. However, the temperature rarely gets cold enough to snow.

Though this oceanic climate applies to most of central France, in the northeastern areas, the weather is affected more by winds coming from over the land. This continental climate results in cold winters and hot summers. Snowstorms are not uncommon in this part of the country, and in cities like Strasbourg. Once winter is over, frequent thunderstorms bring heavy precipitation as temperatures rise and summer comes.

ABOVE: *The south of France enjoys a climate that is hot and dry in summer and warm and wet in winter.*

The Canal du Midi

The Canal du Midi is a 150-mile (240 km) canal in southern France. When built, it was considered one of the greatest construction works of the seventeenth century.

Spanning the regions of the Languedoc-Roussillon and Midi-Pyrenees, the Canal du Midi boasts some unique and truly breathtaking landscapes. The canal passes through a great number of wine growing areas, including the Hérault, the Aude, Minervois, and Corbières. It is famous for its route through little villages and countryside where a wide variety of wildlife can be seen.

A third climate, which affects mainly southern France, is the Mediterranean climate. This results in a much warmer climate than in the rest of France, with mild, wet winters and hot, dryer summers. Mistrals, cool, dry winds that blow from the north—can sometimes bring cooler weather during the winters, but for the most part, the temperature stays between 35° and 50°F (2° to 10°C) even in the coldest months. The summers are another story, with temperatures reaching 84°F (29°C). This climate also affects the island of Corsica, which is considered to be a part of France.

In the mountains like the Alps and the Pyrenees, a few areas stay snowy all year long. Many ski resorts have been built there and are popular tourist destinations. While these climates are much more severe than what is found in the rest of France, they are not widespread, and are contained to the more mountainous areas.

Waterways

France has many important rivers. One of these, the Seine, provides a water route to and from the city of Paris, and then flows into the Atlantic Ocean. Another river, the Loire, is the longest river in France. Because its water level changes often, floods are not uncommon.

ABOVE: The river Seine flowing past Les Andelys in Normandy.

While both of these rivers flow entirely in France, other bodies of water cross the country's borders as well. One of these, the river Rhône, travels from Switzerland to the Mediterranean Sea, and is the largest river in France. The Rhine also originates in the Swiss Alps and forms part of the border between France and Germany. It then flows from Germany to the Netherlands and into the North Sea.

A network of canals connects all France's waterways, most of which are **navigable**. There are not many lakes, but one, Lake Geneva, is on the border between France and Switzerland.

ABOVE: *The river Rhône flowing past the Palace of the Popes in Avignon.*

ABOVE: *Alpine ibex grazing high up in the French Alps with Mont Blanc in the background.*

Fauna and Flora

France has been settled for centuries, long before Europeans ever set foot on North America. Because of this, many of the indigenous species that once inhabited the land have become extinct through human interference. However, the country has made efforts in recent years to conserve the remaining wilderness.

Vegetation varies with the different climates, which often depend on the elevation. At the top of the mountains, barely below the snow line, the only plant life is **lichens** and mosses, clinging tenaciously to the more sheltered rocks. As one descends, alpine pastures become visible. Here, sheep and goats graze during the warmer months.

Otter

Once a rare sight in many parts of France, the otter is making a comeback in some areas thanks to conservation measures. Its strongholds are nevertheless still in remote areas, such as the Atlantic coast and in the Massif Central. Once persecuted for depleting fish stocks, the otter is now protected by law. Otters are shy, nocturnal creatures, perfectly adapted to a life spent hunting in and around water. Webbed feet enable them to swim well in pursuit of fish prey, especially eels, although they also eat crustaceans and aquatic insects. Although often considered to be riverside animals, otters are frequently seen hunting by the sides of lakes and on the seashore, where crabs and other shellfish form an important part of their diet.

After the fields above the **timberline**, a coniferous forest grows up. Trees like fir, larch, and spruce can be found here. At the bottom of the mountain is a deciduous forest. Once covering most of the lower mountains and plains, this forest is now restricted to very limited areas, the land once filled with oak and chestnut trees is now used for farmland.

Evidence of ancient human settlement is also apparent in the Mediterranean area. What was once covered in various types of vegetation like oaks and grasses has been reduced to bare ground through ages of burning, woodcutting, and overgrazing. However, some plants still exist, such as the olive, oak, and pine trees. The dense scrubland characteristic of this region is often referred to as maquis.

When France's woodlands were destroyed, many native animal species found themselves without homes. Many species of deer and fox, as well as wild boar, are still hunted and survive in large numbers only in the deepest forest areas. The chamois, a type of goat, is found in the mountainous areas. There are also smaller animals like the squirrel, and marten, as well as many endangered species like beavers, otters, and lynx that still make their home in France.

Not only mammals but other animals as well make this country their home. Birds like ducks and geese spend the winters here before migrating to cooler climates for the summer. There are also many more exotic birds such as the flamingo and heron that live in the warmer Mediterranean region. While there are some reptiles, they are rare, and few are poisonous. The only poisonous reptile in France is the adder, a species of snake.

Text-Dependent Questions

1. Who are France's neighbors?

2. What is the climate like in the Mediterranean region?

3. What are some of the trees that grow in the Mediterranean region?

Research Project

Make a map showing the geography and major cities of France.

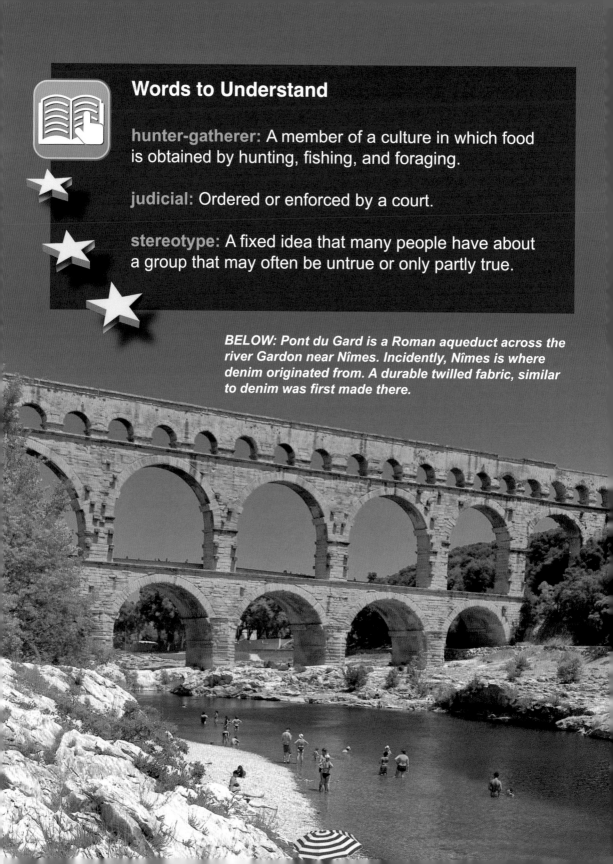

Words to Understand

hunter-gatherer: A member of a culture in which food is obtained by hunting, fishing, and foraging.

judicial: Ordered or enforced by a court.

stereotype: A fixed idea that many people have about a group that may often be untrue or only partly true.

BELOW: Pont du Gard is a Roman aqueduct across the river Gardon near Nîmes. Incidently, Nîmes is where denim originated from. A durable twilled fabric, similar to denim was first made there.

Chapter Two
THE GOVERNMENT & HISTORY OF FRANCE

France has not always been the strong political power it is today. Throughout the ages, the land has been controlled by various groups has and been the site of many bloody battles over its territories. Since prehistoric times, many different peoples have wanted to live in this fertile land.

Prehistoric France

The first inhabitants of France, were **hunter-gatherers** traveling from place to place in search of food. These Stone Age tribes left behind evidence of their existence in the form of cave paintings. These drawings, found throughout the

ABOVE: *A prehistoric wall painting featuring animals in the Lascaux Cave, Vézère Valley, Dordogne. The cave has been designated a UNESCO World Heritage Site.*

THE GOVERNMENT & HISTORY OF FRANCE

Educational Video

A video about the prehistoric cave paintings at Lascaux.

ABOVE: *Carnac is the site of more than 10,000 Neolithic standing stones, also known as menhirs. The stones were hewn from local rock and erected by the pre-Celtic people of Brittany. Some of the stones date back to 4500 BCE.*

24

Pyrenees, but most notably in the Lascaux Caves, show the surprising technological advancement of the people of that time. Contrary to the stereotypes of cavemen as lumbering, uncoordinated, almost monkey-like creatures, the amazing drawings on the cave walls show that the inhabitants of the area had fine motor skills and used forethought and creativity in planning their art. They also used tools like fine brushes and made paints to create these detailed drawings of animals and people.

By 6000 BCE, groups of settlers began to replace the migratory cultures in what is now France. These new peoples built a culture based on agriculture and farming, starting the process that would eventually change the country's landscape forever. Because this way of life was easier than how people had lived previously and could support more life, the population started to grow, increasing from four to five million by 1000 BCE. It was also around this time that metalworking was introduced, leading to the use of metals in such things as cooking pots and other tools.

Dating Systems and Their Meaning

You might be accustomed to seeing dates expressed with the abbreviations BC or AD, as in the year 1000 BC or the year AD 1900. For centuries, this dating system has been the most common in the Western world. However, since BC and AD are based on Christianity (BC stands for Before Christ and AD stands for anno Domini, Latin for "in the year of our Lord"), many people now prefer to use abbreviations that people from all religions can be comfortable using. The abbreviations BCE (meaning Before Common Era) and CE (meaning Common Era) mark time in the same way (for example, 1000 BC is the same year as 1000 BCE, and AD 1900 is the same year as 1900 CE), but BCE and CE do not have the same religious overtones as BC and AD.

ABOVE: *The Roman Triumphal Arch at Orange, in southeastern France, is a UNESCO World Heritage Site and one of the finest examples of Roman architecture in France.*

Around 700 BCE, tribes from the north started invading the land. The largest group was the Celts, who spread throughout France, intermarrying and assimilating into the cultures that were already living there. Remnants of Celtic culture are still evident. For example, Gaul, a former name of what is now France, is derived from a Celtic word meaning "hero."

The Roman Empire

In the first century BCE, the Roman Empire conquered what is now France. The Romans organized their new holdings much as they did the rest of their empire, setting in place a judicial system as well as administration. Cities sprang up as a transportation system was established and the economy expanded. These cities were based on Rome itself and contained such buildings as temples, public baths, and marketplaces, some of which still survive.

As the cities spread their Roman culture to the more rural areas, Latin gradually replaced Gaulish as the country's language. Religious practices changed as well, with Roman cults replacing the Druids and Celtic religions. In 100 CE, Christianity began to spread throughout France, at first only in the cities, which were each under the control of a bishop, but later taking root throughout the country. However, government officials discouraged and even repressed the practice of Christianity.

The Fall of the Roman Empire

Germanic tribes like the Franks and the Alemanni began to take over areas of Roman Gaul in the third century. At first, this seemed like a good thing for the failing empire, as the flow of Germanic peoples to the province brought new laborers and provided a new workforce. However, not all of these groups were content to enter the land peacefully, and the Romans were forced to ally with tribes like the Franks, Burgundians, and Visigoths in the fifth century. While this prevented the immediate collapse of the empire, it weakened it, and gradually the Romans lost power.

Although Gaul was now under Germanic control, its Roman occupation would have a lasting impact on the country. It was the first time the country was united under one government. The Romans had founded many cities, including Paris.

Abbey of Cluny

This historical abbey in Burgundy was the center of the great reforming movement in monasticism in the eleventh century and was one of the most influential places in Europe. It was virtually independent of any secular authority, and its church, the largest in Christendom, with its huge basilica and vast cluster of towers and chapels, must have had a dizzying effect on pilgrims setting eyes on it for the first time.

The abbey was originally founded in 910 and built in its final (the second or third rebuilding) form between 1088, when the foundation stone was laid by the Pope's emissary, and 1130. The finely ordered Burgundian Romanesque style that it typified was to be echoed, even imitated, in later Cluniac houses and can be seen today, especially on the pilgrims' route to Santiago de Compostela, in Spain, which Cluny supported.

According to Abbot Hugh, the abbey was built at the direction of St. Peter and St. Paul, who outlined its dimensions on the ground with a long rope. The speed with which the buildings were completed confirms that Cluny was extremely well endowed, as the costs must have been enormous.

Today it is possible to trace the outline of the original abbey on the ground; but of the actual structure, all that remains besides traces of the basilica is one solitary tower and the south transept. The abbey was badly damaged in the French Wars of Religion and closed during the Revolution. The building was then demolished.

Modern-day highways are built on old Roman roads, leading to some confusion as some roads seem to meander aimlessly through cities and the countryside. Even the French language is based on Latin, although there are some Germanic and other influences apparent.

The Middle Ages

The movement of these Germanic tribes into France marked the beginning of a period known as the Middle Ages. During the early period of this era, from about 350 to 1050, the state of the country declined;

ABOVE: Martin Luther (1529) by Lucas Cranach the Elder.

literacy, trade, and the legal system all deteriorated. However, not all aspects of life suffered. Many minorities achieved more rights during this era. Women were given the ability to maintain more control of property, and Jews, who had been persecuted under the Romans, were treated better under the Germanic kings.

Eventually, the Franks conquered the region that had once been Gaul and again gave it a more centralized government. Led by Clovis, King of the Franks, this group conquered much of present-day Germany and southeastern France. Clovis, realizing the importance of religion, converted to Catholic Christianity. At a time when most kings practiced Arianism, a type of Christianity not recognized by his choice the Catholic Church, made Clovis more agreeable to the pope, as well as making him more popular among his Christian subjects. His precedent led to centuries of rulers using Catholicism to aid them in their goals as leaders.

The Reformation

In 1517, Martin Luther began an attempt to reform the Catholic Church. This German theologian started a new Christian belief system, Protestantism. In France, this new movement took many forms, the most popular one based on the teachings of John Calvin, a French humanist. The growing Protestant communities came to be known as Huguenots.

The government had mixed feelings about this new movement. Francis I, the monarch at the time, at first protected people suspected of being Protestants. As time went on, however, he eventually became more suspicious and less accepting of them. In the 1540s, thousands were tried and either put to death or sentenced to spend the rest of their lives rowing the galleys.

At the same time, the Counter-Reformation traveled throughout France. This movement inspired reform of the existing Catholic Church, including the clergy and the development of new movements within the Church. Its goal was to again unite the nation under one faith—Catholicism.

In 1598, Henry IV issued the Edict of Nantes. This gave Protestants the right to practice their faith—under certain conditions. It also allowed them to have control of a few cities. However, this bill was so controversial that it was not registered for months. In the end, the edict did nothing to bring peace between the Protestants and Catholics. All it did was maintain the struggle at a less violent level.

The Enlightenment

The 1700s brought an increase in France's literacy rate. This helped bring about the Enlightenment, a period of growth that brought new ideas and concepts to the country. This movement was led by the *philosophes*, a group of scientists and thinkers who worked toward reform. They wrote pamphlets and books, the best known of which is the *Encyclopédie*, an international best seller.

Although these people worked together, they all had very different ideas about politics, agreeing only on the fact that liberty and freedom were desirable. Some, like Charles-Louis de Montesquieu, believed this was most easily brought

ABOVE: *Henry IV of France.*

31

about through protecting the rights of the people as individuals. Voltaire represented another group, those who thought a strong monarchy could be used to bring about freedom. Some of the more radical, like philosopher Jean-Jacques Rousseau, believed a democracy should be established and the monarchy abolished altogether. These new thinkers were part of what led to the French Revolution.

The French Revolution

Many factors caused the French Revolution. Among them was the fact that the king did not inspire much respect. Louis XV took little interest in the state of the country, leaving all the administrative decisions to his advisers. Instead, he seemed content to devote his attention to his many mistresses, especially the Marquise de Pompadour, who he refused to give up even when urged

ABOVE: *Jean-Jacques Rousseau by Maurice Quentin de La Tour.*

to by the court. Even after his death, the monarchy remained weak, with his son Louis XVI's only triumph being the American Revolution. Add this to the ideas spread by the Enlightenment and the hope for freedom inspired by the successful American Revolution, and the stage was set for change.

In 1788, the Estates-General voted to give an equal vote to each estate of the realm, instead of basing it on the number of people in each estate. The Third Estate, which was formed from commoners and had the greatest number of representatives, saw this as an attempt to take power from them and give more to the First Estate (the nobles) and the Second Estate (the clergy). After arguing over this issue for weeks, the Third Estate struck out on its own, forming a new parliament it called the National Assembly in June. The other two estates were invited to join, as long as they agreed to vote by head instead of

ABOVE: *Louis XV of France by Hyacinthe Rigaud.*

estate, and a crisis was averted. However, this break from tradition made the king look bad as he searched for a way to gain control over the situation.

Tensions deepened as a famine took hold in France. Peasants couldn't afford food as prices, especially that of bread, kept rising and rising. Finally, desperate Parisians attacked the Bastille on July 14, 1789, a day now celebrated as a national holiday in France. The Bastille, an old prison, served as a symbol of the monarchy and everything that the people wanted to put down. The French Revolution had begun.

The French Revolution caused more problems than had been anticipated. The government changed completely, and revolution became almost acceptable in the political arena. Because of this, a peaceful end was harder to reach than had been expected.

In 1789, France started its journey to recovery. To this end, the Declaration of the Rights of Man and of the Citizen was written. This was the beginning of a

ABOVE: *Versailles was the seat of political power in the Kingdom of France from 1682, when King Louis XIV moved the royal court from Paris. In 1789 the royal family was forced to return to the capital in October.*

constitution, finished in 1791, that enforced a limited monarchy and put most authority in the hands of a unicameral legislature.

During this time, a mob of upset citizens forced the royal family to leave the palace at Versailles and remain in Paris, where the king was made to accept the reforms of the people. In 1791, the king and his family tried to escape but were stopped at the border of France, where they were returned to Paris, virtually prisoners.

A new legislative body, the National Convention, voted to end the monarchy in 1792. In its place was to be a republic. The king was tried and put to death in January 1793.

Not all was peaceful among the members of the National Convention. In 1793, Maximilien Robespierre and his following of radical Jacobeans took over the parliament and started the Reign of Terror, a time meant to force citizens to help the republic. Over a quarter of a million people were arrested and more than 30,000 guillotined, often for the most trivial of reasons or because they were alleged to have worked against the republic. Eventually, they had so alienated the remainder of France that Robespierre and his advisers were executed, ending the Reign of Terror.

For the first time since the Revolution a more moderate government was put in place. A new convention worked to perpetuate the accomplishments of the Revolution, while keeping an event like the Terror from ever happening again. To this end, a bicameral legislature was established as well as an executive branch consisting of five members known as the Directory. Although this system worked for a while, it was ultimately unsuccessful, setting the stage for the next period in France's history: the rule of Napoleon Bonaparte.

ABOVE: *Maximilien Robespierre.*

ABOVE: Napoleon Bonaparte on the Bridge at Arcole *by Antoine-Jean Gros.*

Napoleon Bonaparte

In 1799, Napoleon and his troops attacked the government and replaced it with one of their own devising, called the Consulate. It consisted of Bonaparte and two others, but Napoleon was the one really in charge. After reforming the government, he declared himself emperor, and the country was back to where it had been before the Revolution.

At its height, Napoleon's First Empire stretched from Poland to Spain, and was allied with Russia, Prussia, and Austria. However, it didn't last long, as countries that had become used to independence rebelled. Perhaps one of Napoleon's biggest mistakes and one that led to his downfall was his attack of Russia in 1812, a mistake later repeated by Adolf Hitler during World War II. Caught in the middle of a Russian winter, Napoleon's troops quickly ran out of food and supplies; wagons were unable to get to them. The French troops never came into armed conflict with the Russians—the native troops retreated, burning any towns and cities that might have proved useful to the French. After thousands of his soldiers died from starvation and exposure, Napoleon was forced to admit defeat without reaching his destination of Moscow. By 1814, Napoleon was forced to abdicate his throne when armies invaded France. He was exiled to the island of Elba.

The year after, Napoleon tried to return. He came back to France, and for a short time, known as the Hundred Days, Napoleon gathered the people to him with talk of a more left-wing regime. However, at the Battle of Waterloo, Napoleon was defeated again. This time he was exiled to the island of Saint Helena, where he died in 1821.

The Industrial Revolution

Unlike Great Britain, where the change from household industries to factories seemed to occur almost overnight, France's Industrial Revolution was more gradual. For many years, France lagged behind countries like Germany and Britain. Not only had France just emerged from decades of revolutions, but it did not have as great a population growth as did other countries. One of the reasons for this was that the peasant class, almost extinct in other European countries, was still around. Because they were poor, their family size was limited, meaning a lower birthrate. Therefore, there was less demand for more goods because there were fewer people to ask for them, leaving no need for better, quicker ways of production.

The Industrial Revolution started in the textile industry, as it did in many other countries. However, in the 1840s, the railway industry brought a boom throughout the economy. This also increased a demand for mining and metal ores to make rails. The Revolution eventually led to the development of a middle class, who worked mainly in small shops and professional jobs.

World War I

France's involvement in World War I began in 1914, when German troops came through Belgium, looking to take control of Paris and defeat the French troops trying to retake Alsace-Lorraine from Germany. France's success in keeping the Germans from accomplishing their goals may have been the factor that kept the other side from winning quickly. Instead, a stalemate resulted that lasted for years, with neither side gaining much territory. The only result was the loss of millions of lives.

The Treaty of Versailles, which ended the war, dictated the terms of peace. France

ABOVE: *French soldiers posing in a trench on June 16, 1917.*

37

ABOVE: *Hitler's armies attacked France in 1940 and then occupied it.*

regained control of Alsace-Lorraine, and Germany was forced to pay reparations for the war. Germany also had to agree to demilitarize the area between France and Germany known as the Rhineland, which France could occupy until 1935.

World War I led to another decline in France's birthrate as millions of men returned home wounded or, worse, didn't return home at all. Immigrants came into the country to take the jobs left behind by the lost soldiers. During the war, women had been allowed to work in factories, but were now pushed out of their jobs to make room for veterans. There were also economic losses as the area that Germany had taken over contained more than half of the country's steel and coal industries. Coupled with the economic cost of the war itself, debt increased and the value of the franc weakened.

In 1928, France joined the League of Nations in an attempt to stave off another war. However, this organization was weak and had no real power, partly because the United States refused to join.

World War II

In 1939, after numerous German violations of the Treaty of Versailles, and despite the League of Nations' attempts at appeasement, France and Britain declared war on Germany. Despite this, the French took no action at first. Then, in 1940, Hitler attacked and invaded France. Unlike what had happened in World War I, this was a decisive victory for Germany, and France became an occupied country.

In 1918, France had signed an armistice saying that they would demobilize their armed forces, basically giving over the northern two-thirds of the country to Germany. Despite ceding to all of Germany's demands, the country still suffered. Thousands of forced laborers worked in Germany, and the country was forced to give money to help support the German war effort. In 1942, Germany took control over the remainder of France, resulting in a French puppet government.

Vichy, the government at the time, was almost as bad as the Germans. Although the regime was not actively involved in genocide, anti-Semitism was rampant, and Jews were forced to give up their jobs and property. Some Jews were sent to Germany where they were placed in death camps.

Although most people supported the French government at first, people began resisting German control. Charles de Gaulle, the former undersecretary of war, escaped to Paris, where he formed a government-in-exile. Groups of people fought against the Germans, sabotaging the war effort and secretly communicating with de Gaulle. The were known as the French Resistance.

France was liberated in 1944 after Allied troops landed at Normandy. A new provisional government, led by de Gaulle, assumed power.

France and the Rest of the World

France today is one of the most modern countries in the world and is a leader among European nations. It plays an influential global role as a permanent member of the United Nations Security Council, the North Atlantic Treaty Organization (NATO), the G7, the G20, the European Union, and other multilateral organizations. In recent decades, its reconciliation and cooperation with Germany have proved central to the economic integration of Europe, including the introduction of a common currency, the euro.

ABOVE: Charles de Gaulle.

France's Government Today

France's modern government consists of a republic led by a president, much like the United States. The current form of government was established with a new constitution in 1958, one that gave more power to the president and less to parliament.

The president is elected by popular vote; there is no electoral college as in the United States. The president is the head of state and of the country, but he must appoint a prime minister who takes over the task of controlling the government. The legislative branch of the government is bicameral: parliament is made up of the National Assembly and the Senate, which has slightly less influence. There is also the Constitutional Council, a judicial branch of the government that supervises elections and decides the constitutionality of laws.

ABOVE: *The Palais Bourbon, where the National Assembly meets.*

Amendments to the constitution may come about in many different ways. The president can propose an amendment, or the government or members of parliament may request one. However the amendment is proposed, it must have the approval of both branches of parliament and be approved in a referendum.

There are three levels of local government: communes, departments, and regions. Communes are the smallest and can range in size from one small village to a portion of a larger city. Then there are departments, most of them named after the geographical area in which they lie. These departments make up the regions, the largest divisions of local government. No matter what the size, all of these have their own elected legislative and executive branches.

Text-Dependent Questions

1. What religion did Martin Luther attempt to reform in 1517?

2. Who was Maximilien Robespierre?

3. When was France finally liberated during World War II?

 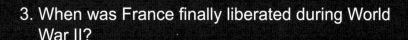

Research Project

Write a one-page biography on Napoleon Bonaparte.

The Formation of the European Union (EU)

The EU is a confederation of European nations that continues to grow. As of 2017, there are twenty-eight official members. Several other candidates are also waiting for approval. All countries that enter the EU agree to follow common laws about foreign security policies. They also agree to cooperate on legal matters that go on within the EU. The European Council meets to discuss all international matters and make decisions about them. Each country's own concerns and interests are important, though. And apart from legal and financial issues, the EU tries to uphold values such as peace, human dignity, freedom, and equality.

All member countries remain autonomous. This means that they generally keep their own laws and regulations. The idea for a union among European nations was first mentioned after World War II. The war had devastated much of Europe, both physically and financially. In 1950, the French foreign minister suggested that France and West Germany combine their coal and steel industries under one authority. Both countries would have control over the

ABOVE: *The entrance to the European Union Parliament Building in Brussels.*

Member Countries

Austria	Greece	Romania
Belgium	Hungary	Slovakia
Bulgaria	Ireland	Slovenia
Croatia	Italy	Spain
Cyprus	Latvia	Sweden
Czech Republic	Lithuania	United Kingdom
Denmark	Luxembourg	*(Brexit: For the time*
Estonia	Malta	*being, the United*
Finland	Netherlands	*Kingdom remains a full*
France	Poland	*member of the EU.)*
Germany	Portugal	

industries. This would help them become more financially stable. It would also make war between the countries much more difficult. The idea was interesting to other European countries as well. In 1951, France, West Germany, Belgium, Luxembourg, the Netherlands, and Italy signed the Treaty of Paris, creating the European Coal and Steel Community. These six countries would become the core of the EU.

In 1957, these same countries signed the Treaties of Rome, creating the European Economic Community. In 1965, the Merger Treaty formed the European Community. Finally, in 1992, the Maastricht Treaty was signed. This treaty defined the European Union. It gave a framework for expanding the EU's political role, particularly in the area of foreign and security policy. It would also replace national currencies with the euro. The next year, the treaty went into effect. At that time, the member countries included the original six plus another six who had joined during the 1970s and '80s.

In the following years, the EU would take more steps to form a single market for its members. This would make joining the union even more advantageous. In addition to enlargement, the EU is steadily becoming more integrated through its own policies for closer cooperation between member states.

Words to Understand

capital: Accumulated assets (as money) invested or available for investment.

modernize: To make (something) modern and more suited to present needs.

nationalize: To invest control or ownership of in the national government.

BELOW: Vineyard in the famous wine-making region of Beaujolais.

Chapter Three
THE FRENCH ECONOMY

While French industry mainly consisted of farms and small businesses until the 1940s, after World War II the government set in place a plan designed to **modernize** the economy. These reforms were designed to **nationalize** different industries, including energy production, the banking system, and many factories and other manufacturing fields. This, along with France's induction into the the European Community—the forerunner of the EU—led to a period of economic growth over the past twenty-five years. Today,

ABOVE: *France's automotive industry is a vital part of its economy.*

France boasts the world's sixth-strongest economy, behind only the United States, China, Japan, Germany, and the United Kingdom.

As of 2016, France's gross domestic product (GDP) was equivalent to 2.48 trillion U.S. dollars. Per capita income is US$42,400. Though this may seem like a lot of money, not everyone earns this much. This is an average figure—the average amount an average French citizen earns in a year; many people earn far below this amount, while others earn much more.

ABOVE: *La Défense is the financial district of Paris.*

Perfume Manufacturing

When it comes to the art of perfume-making, no country ranks more highly than France. Many of the greatest names in the perfume industry, such as Chanel, Christian Dior, or Givenchy, are French. In terms of international perfume sales, France is leader, with 30 percent of the world market. Perfume is one of France's top ten exports, with sales and distribution all over the world.

Entrance into the EU

The creation of the EU put in place a single market in Europe for producers to sell their goods and services. Though this has allowed people, **capital**, and goods to move freely throughout Europe, there have been some downfalls. French businesses, used to protection by trade barriers, have had to become more competitive in order to survive in the wider marketplace.

The formation of the EU also brought about the adoption of the euro. This common currency makes it even easier for people and goods to travel from one country to another.

Socialism in France

Various French governments have tried different variations of government control of the economy. In 1982, François Mitterrand, then the president of the country, attempted to nationalize most of the economy. At the height of this socialist plan, the state owned thirteen out of twenty of the major corporations in France.

ABOVE: *France has a healthy tourism industry, with all-year appeal. Tourists can choose from a city break in any one of France's beautiful cities, to skiing in winter, or a sunshine vacation in the south.*

Since then, the government has begun to encourage limited privatization of businesses. Now France tends toward a mixed economy, a system in which both government and private sectors share control of various industries.

Although there is some private ownership of goods and services in the economy, the government is still involved, using its influence to make sure the economy is growing and stable. France used fiscal policies, such as cutting taxes and increasing government spending, to increase demand for goods by giving people more money to spend and therefore encouraging the economy to grow. However, this policy often results in a budget deficit, with the government spending more than it takes in. In 2017 France's national audit office said the country's budget deficit could stand above the EU limit of 3 percent for the 10th consecutive year.

Taxes and Other Income

The French government gets income from many sources, including taxes. Things like sales tax and income tax provide the government with money. There is also a wealth tax in France, which those with assets worth more than €800,000 must pay. All in all, France is one of the most heavily taxed nations in the EU.

A large part of the GDP comes from government expenditure. Social security, the wages of government employees, debt service on the national debt, and investment all contribute to the money people make from the federal government.

Educational Video

Argeville: A famous fragrance manufacturer from Grasse— a town in the heart of the perfume industry.

ABOVE: *The Mediterranean summer climate makes the south of France a popular destination for holiday makers, who visit towns such as Nice, Juan le Pins, and Cannes.*

The Labor Force

The structure of the economy has changed drastically in recent years. In the 1950s, most French workers had jobs in agriculture or industry. Now, however, the service sector is the most popular, employing 78.8 percent of France's labor force of 30.5 million people. The highest numbers of new jobs are in the education, health, and public administration fields.

Economic Sectors

France is the EU's leading producer of agricultural goods, with more than 48.4 million acres (19.6 million hectares) used for farming. The country produces dairy products, beef, wheat, oilseeds, fruits and vegetables, and wine.

The reason France is able to produce so many different products is because the country is so well suited to agriculture. There is fertile soil, plentiful rain, and a long growing season. The variety comes from regional differences in climate—in the northwest, where it is cooler and wetter, there are grasslands for cattle to graze on, while in the Mediterranean region, where it is warm and dry, it is easy to grow various types of grapes.

The Common Agricultural Policy was put in place in 1957 with the creation of the European Economic Community. This created a system of common prices across what is now the EU, leading to greater agricultural production and

Educational Video

A journey through the wine regions of Bordeaux.

ABOVE: *The warm and sunny weather in Provence is suitable for growing lavender for the perfume industry.*

helping many farmers improve their incomes. Because France is the leading agricultural country in the EU, it benefits the most from these funds.

France also is a mining country, the second-largest producer of iron ore in Western Europe. This was once a major source of employment, but production decreased when it was discovered that French iron has many impurities. However, other metals and minerals—such as uranium, aluminum, salt, gypsum, tungsten, and sulfur—are still mined. Coal is also mined, although on a much smaller scale than at the turn of the twentieth century. There are also stone quarries that provide such materials as sand, gravel, stone, and clay.

Manufacturing is another major industry in France. It accounts for the main source of income through exports and produces such goods as food products, automobiles, airplanes, ships, trains, machinery, chemicals, and textiles. The country is well known for its innovations in the transportation sectors; the French TGV (*Train à Grande Vitesse* or "Train of Great Speed") is one of the world's fastest passenger trains.

People from all over the world come to France to visit, making tourism an important part of the service sector. In 2016, France was the most visited country in the world, with more than 82.6 million people coming to see this beautiful and historic nation. The French themselves travel around their own country, taking advantage of the five-week paid vacation all French workers must receive, to experience a different part of France.

ABOVE: *France is most famous for its fine wines and cheeses. The export market for both is very important to the French economy. The best produce is protected by law.*

The Economy of France

Gross Domestic Product (GDP): US$2.73 trillion
GDP Per Capita: US$42,400
Industries: machinery, chemicals, automobiles, metallurgy, aircraft, electronics; textiles, food processing; tourism
Agriculture: wheat, cereals, sugar beets, potatoes, wine grapes; beef, dairy products; fish
Export Commodities: machinery and transportation equipment, aircraft, plastics, chemicals, pharmaceutical products, iron and steel, beverages
Export Partners: Germany 16.1%, Spain 7.5%, U.S. 7.4%, Italy 7.3%, UK 7%, Belgium 6.8%
Import Commodities: machinery and equipment, vehicles, crude oil, aircraft, plastics, chemicals
Import Partners: Germany 16.9%, China 9.1%, Italy 7.5%, Belgium 6.7%, Spain 6.4%, Netherlands 6%, UK 4.3%
Currency: euro

Source: www.cia.gov 2017.

Transportation

France enjoys a well-maintained network of highways, railroads, and waterways. The country's dense system of roads makes it home to one of the best transportation systems in the world. It was the first country in the EU to have fast railroads available for passengers. The metro systems in the cities, most notably Paris, are easy to use and very comfortable.

Paris is the center of the transportation system. It is home to a major airport—Charles de Gaulle—and all of France's major roads and waterways

ABOVE: *A high-speed train SNCF TGV Duplex between Paris and Marseilles. Train travel in France is subsidized by the government, which makes it affordable.*

lead from the city. Recently, however, efforts have been made to connect other larger cities while skipping Paris.

France has more than 5,300 miles (8,500 kilometers) of navigable rivers and canals, making it the longest system of water transportation in Europe. Because most of these canals were built in the 1800s and today's large ships cannot fit in them, water transport of goods has decreased in recenct decades as other alternatives, such as air transportation, have become cheaper and easier. There are many seaports in France, such as those at Marseille and Le Havre, which are the entry points for the country's imports of petroleum.

Energy

France has few natural energy resources of its own, relying mainly on imported petroleum. While the country was able to mine coal during the Industrial Revolution, this power source was quickly outdated as gasoline developed, and gasoline is a scarce commodity in France. In 1973, the oil crisis showed the pitfalls of depending on foreign oil, and the government started developing alternative energy sources.

France found that it could use nuclear power to make its own energy, thereby reducing the amount it needed to import from other countries. France's nuclear power plants produces 78.5 percent of its power; after the United States, France is the largest producer of nuclear power plants. While this has met with few protests, not all attempts to harness this type of power have been successful. In southeastern France, a plant was closed in 1998 after technical problems and safety concerns, along with protests from various environmental groups. Looking ahead, the French government has pledged to reduce the amount of nuclear power it generates.

ABOVE: *France's large population relies heavily on nuclear power for its energy needs.*

Not all of France's electricity comes from nuclear power; the country also uses hydroelectric and thermal power. France produces more energy than it needs, exporting the excess to the countries around it, such as the UK, Italy, and Switzerland.

Economic Problems

While France has a strong economy, the country still has many problems. One of these is the high unemployment rate. From the mid-1970s, the number of people without jobs has been consistently about 10 percent, falling slightly to 9.5 percent in 2017. While some unemployment is necessary, and even helpful to the economy, the rate of full employment is usually considered around 5

ABOVE: *Lac de Cap de Long in the French Hautes-Pyrenees. This is the site of a huge dam that generates hydroelectricity.*

percent—half that of France. France has taken many measures to lower unemployment, but with limited success; among these efforts was a law that reduced the workweek from thirty-nine to thirty-five hours (which means that more workers would be needed to accomplish the same tasks, creating more jobs).

Because the economy is not growing very fast, it is getting harder and harder for France to maintain its welfare system, which has traditionally been extremely generous to its citizens. France is finding it necessary to reform this system, delicately balancing the benefits each person may receive with a solution that is agreeable to the public.

France has come a long way since its economy consisted mostly of family farms. However, some things don't change; France is still a farming country, producing the most agricultural goods in Western Europe.

Text-Dependent Questions

1. Where does the French economy rank when compared to the rest of the world?

2. What is France's GDP?

3. How important is nuclear power in France?

Research Project

Write a brief report on France's agriculture.

Words to Understand

dialect: A regional variety of language distinguished by features of vocabulary, grammar, and pronunciation.

immigrants: A people who come to a country to take up permanent residence.

minorites: Members of a section of a population differing from others in some characteristics and often subjected to differential treatment.

BELOW: The harbor town of Dunkerque is the most northerly French town near the Belgian border. The main language spoken here is Flemish, a dialect of Dutch.

Chapter Four
CITIZENS OF FRANCE:
PEOPLE, CUSTOMS & CULTURE

France is home to 64,836,154 people, making it the fourth most populated nation in Europe. While many people live here, it is also the largest nation in Western Europe, meaning that the population density is still less than in most European nations, with 288 people per square mile (111 people per square kilometer).

Ethnicities

Although most people in the country are French citizens, they have varied ethnic backgrounds. Hundreds of years of invading groups have left their mark, including the Romans, Celts, and Franks, from whom the name France comes.

The French government has tried hard to assimilate minorities and has come a long way from the French Revolution, when less than half of the people spoke French. After the Revolution, in an attempt to find unity, the government declared that if a person lived in France, they were French. This was part of the government's effort to make a nation based on a common language. This worked until the formation of the EU, which forced France for the first time to acknowledge and offer rights to minorities.

Many ethnic minorities are descended from ancient peoples and live on the same land their ancestors have inhabited for centuries. For example, in the northern part of France live a group called the Flemings, who live around the town of Dunkerque. They speak mainly a dialect of Dutch and have assimilated without protest into French culture. On the other hand, the Bretons, who have Celtic blood and live in Brittany, seek to have their own culture and way of life. To this extent they differentiate themselves from the French by incorporating their Celtic heritage into their lives and setting up schools that use their own language.

ABOVE: *In Carcassonne in the Languedoc-Roussillon region of southern France the Occitan language is spoken by about 610,000 people.*

Educational Video

Ten interesting facts about the history of France, its customs, and places to visit.

Immigrants from all over the world make up approximately 7.5 percent of France's population. The largest immigrant group is from North Africa, including the Islamic nations of Algeria, Morocco, and Tunisia. There are more than 4 million Muslims in France, many from Africa or Turkey and who live in France's cities. This has led to much debate as people argue over whether or not traditional Islamic head coverings should be allowed. In 2011, a law was passed forbidding full-face coverings in public; many Muslims felt the law was unfairly targeting them.

Language

French is the official language of France. The language is a **dialect** of the ancient *langue d'oïl*, which originated in what is now northern France. Other, regional languages are spoken as well, the most widespread of which is Occitan, the *langue d'oc* (Languedoc), which is spoken mainly in southern France. Almost 6 million speak Provençal, the major dialect. However, most people speak mainstream French as well.

Other languages include German in the region of Alsace; Breton in Brittany; Catalan and Basque, in the Pyrenees; Flemish, which is based on Dutch; and Corse, an Italian dialect spoken on the island of Corsica. Many of France's immigrants also speak their native languages, most notably Arabic and Turkish.

French Food

It is a not uncommon to see French people sitting at sidewalk cafés, enjoying a cup of coffee or Orangina, a popular French drink, while they watch the passersby or read the paper. These small restaurants are all over France, pointing to the emphasis the culture places on food.

France is famous for its food; the country has many regional dishes that can be found nowhere else in the world. Some of the more popular foods that have become internationally known include: quiches; crêpes; bouillabaisse, a fish soup; and pâté de foie gras, a spread made of goose livers. French bread is also known for its taste; most people go every day to boulangeries to get fresh baked goods.

Unlike Americans, whose largest meal of the day tends to be eaten in the evening, the French eat a small breakfast, a big lunch, and a small dinner. For special occasions, however, huge, multicourse meals are served, lasting from around 8 p.m. until sometimes very early in the morning. These elaborate dinners consist of appetizers, one or two main courses, a salad, fruits and cheeses, and then dessert. Of course, various types of wine are served throughout the meal.

ABOVE: *L'escargot (snails) cooked in butter, garlic, and parsley, is a favorite dish in France.*

Crêpes

Makes 6-8

Ingredients
3 eggs
1 ½ cups milk
1 egg
¾ cup of flour
¾ teaspoon of salt
5 tablespoons melted butter

Directions
Place all the ingredients into a blender and mix on high for one minute. Strain the batter to remove any lumps. Cover the mixture and let it stand for at least an hour. Heat a skillet to a medium heat and brush with the butter. Add ¼ of a cup of batter to the pan, picking the skillet up and swirling it so the bottom is covered with batter. Cook for about 20 seconds or until the underside is golden. Flip the crêpe over to cook on the other side. Turn out onto a plate. Add fillings of your choice, such as jam, ham, cheese, or chocolate. Alternatively, make Crêpes Suzette which uses orange liqueur and oranges.

Croque Monsieur

Makes one sandwich

Ingredients
2 slices of white bread
1 tablespoon butter
1 slice of ham
4 tablespoons oil
2–3 tablespoons of grated Gruyère cheese

Directions
While preheating a skillet to a medium heat, spread the butter on both sides of the bread. Make a sandwich out of the ham and half of the cheese and grill in the skillet as if making a grilled cheese sandwich. Cook one side until it becomes golden brown. Add the rest of the cheese to the top of the sandwich and press down a little so that it sticks, then flip over and cook until the cheese is brown. For a variation, called Croque Madame, fry an egg sunny side up and put it on top of the sandwich.

Religion in France

The most popular religion in France is Roman Catholicism, with a large percentage of the population claiming to practice this faith. However, while many identify with this religion and its culture, only a few—about 5 percent—actively practice it.

Islam is France's second-largest faith, with about 7 to 9 percent of the population Muslim. There are also some Protestants, although they are a minority. Protestants fled France in the sixteenth and seventeenth centuries because of persecution from the Catholics; not many returned. There is also a small Jewish minority. However, the number of French people claiming to have no religion at all is growing year on year.

ABOVE: *The Church of Notre-Dame-de-l'Assomption is a Catholic church in Auvers-sur-Oise, which was famously painted by Vincent van Gogh.*

The government supported both Christianity and Judaism until the beginning of the twentieth century. In 1905, church and state were officially separated. Because many people opposed the Catholic Church and their control over schools and the educational system, the government was forbidden to pay public funds to any religious official or clergy. Therefore, the state cannot officially recognize any religion.

Education

Basic schooling is guaranteed for all French citizens. Students must attend school from ages six to sixteen, and all schools are free. Universities are also free to those students who qualify. There is also an extensive system of private schools, many controlled by the Catholic Church. One out of six children attend these schools.

Education starts out with two or three years of preschool, which is optional. Students go on to a primary, or elementary, school until they are eleven. After the *collège*, or middle school, which students attend until they are fifteen, they go on to *lycée*, or high school. At this point, teens have a choice. There are general schools, which are much like those in the United States, offering a well-rounded education in all the subjects. Students attend these general schools for three years, ending with a nationwide exam. If students pass this exam, they earn the *baccalauréat* diploma needed to enter a university. This is a hard exam; only two-thirds of those who take it pass, and the others must take it over again. Students can also decide to go to a technical or vocational school and earn a professional certificate/diploma after one to three years.

The system of universities is expanding, adding new colleges apart from the general, traditional university. One such type is the technological institutes, or *instituts universitaires de technologie*. They specialize in such fields as engineering and other technology-related majors. Community colleges have also developed in smaller cities and towns.

Besides colleges and universities, there are graduate schools, called *grandes écoles*. These are extremely hard to get into; applicants must pass competitive exams.

Sports

The French people are very active, loving physical activity of all kinds. While professional sports like soccer (called *le foot*) and bicycle racing are extremely popular, many people belong to sports clubs where they play for fun. The most widespread of these clubs allow members to play soccer, tennis, basketball, or *boules*.

The Tour de France is the world's most famous bicycle race. Each year such professionals as Tejay van Garderen gather to compete for the prize. The French Open, one of tennis's Grand Slam events, attracts visitors from around the world to the clay courts of Roland-Garros Stadium in Paris.

ABOVE: *Cyclists at the start of stage 18 of the Tour de France in Briançon.*

ABOVE: *Henri Leconte is a former French professional tennis player. He reached the men's singles final at the French Open in 1988, won the French Open men's doubles title in 1984, and helped France win the Davis Cup in 1991.*

Claude Monet (1840–1926)

Probably the best known and loved of the Impressionist painters, Monet was concerned with light and shade. His painting are suffused with life, vivacity, and movement.

His ambition of documenting the French countryside led him to adopt a method of painting the same scene many times in order to capture the changing of the light and the passing of the seasons. From 1883, Monet lived in Giverny, where he purchased a house and property and began a vast landscaping project that included lily ponds, which would become the subjects of his best-known works. Monet and Impressionism are so interrelated that it seems at times that he must be the only Impressionist, so much does he personify its characteristics and qualities. Of course, a whole art movement cannot be encompassed in the work of one artist, but with Monet at its heart, we can include other important Impressionists such as Renoir, Sisley, and Pissarro, to name but a few.

The Arts: Architecture, Painting, Music, and Literature

France has produced many famous artists, as well as whole movements of painting. One such style is Impressionism, a movement of the late nineteenth and early twentieth centuries. The movement got its name from Claude Monet's painting *Impression, Sunrise*. Although he refused to call himself an Impressionist, one of the first practitioners of the technique was Édouard Manet. Pierre Auguste Renoir is one of Impressionism's most famous artists.

However, French painters have won prestige throughout history, from baroque artists like Georges de la Tour and Claude Lorrain to Romantic painters like Eugène Delacroix. In the twentieth century, Henri Matisse,

Pierre Bonnard, and Marcel Duchamp became famous for their modern works.

Painting is not the only art form at which the French excel. The country is filled with examples of great architecture, some of the earliest examples being its Gothic churches, built between the twelfth and fifteenth centuries. The Palace of Versailles is a great example of the luxury of the neoclassical era, and, of course, the Eiffel Tower shows the talent of the nineteenth-century architect Charles Garnier.

Since the eleventh century, French musicians have been singing of noble deeds and quests in the form of *chansons de geste*. Throughout history France has been home to a vibrant musical tradition, creating new forms of music and raising famous composers. In the fourteenth century, composer Guillaume de

ABOVE: Impression, Sunrise *by Claude Monet; oil on canvas, 1872.*

Machaut developed the polyphonic form of music, or the idea that music could have more than one part. Famous French musicians and composers include Georges Bizet, Camille Saint-Saëns, Gabriel Fauré, and Claude Debussy. The French continue to enjoy music, and newer forms are popular today, including rock and pop hits.

French literature has been world famous for centuries. Writers such as Marcel Proust and Albert Camus continue to be popular. The country is also home to many books for a younger audience; children all over the world read *The Little Prince* by Antoine de Saint Exupéry.

Festivals and Holidays

Because much of French culture is based on Roman Catholicism, many of the holidays celebrated have a religious origin. Christmas and Easter are celebrated much as they are in the United States. However, a festival with a uniquely French flavor is Mardi Gras, or "Fat Tuesday." This is the day before Lent (the forty days preceding Easter) begins and marks the end of the Carnival season. Parades, music, costumes, and food mark the festivities, as people rush to celebrate before the traditional season of fasting and prayer.

The national holiday in France is Bastille Day on July 14. This celebrates the fall of the Bastille and the success of the common

ABOVE: *Georges Bizet.*

ABOVE: *Claude Debussy.*

ABOVE: *Marcel Proust.*

people in the French Revolution. There are many regional festivals, celebrating everything from food to film and from music to another successful harvest.

RIGHT: In the Middle Ages, the Paris Carnival was linked to the popular celebration of the Feast of Fools, which preceded it. It was an important tradition and festive event, involving all social classes. The carnival used to last several months from Epiphany to Lent, with a high point on Fat Tuesday (Mardi Gras). Nowadays, it is a fun procession.

Text-Dependent Questions

1. Where do the Bretons live?

2. What is the most popular religion in France?

3. Where is Monet's house and property?

Research Project

Write a one-page biography on the artist Pierre-Auguste Renoir.

Words to Understand

Candlemas: A church festival, on February 2, in honor of the presentation of Christ in the temple and the purification of the Virgin Mary.

catacombs: A subterranean cemetery with recesses for tombs.

neolithic: Relating to the latest period of the Stone Age.

BELOW: The Paris skyline showing grand buildings along the river Seine. The Eiffel Tower is in the background.

Chapter Five
THE FAMOUS CITIES
OF FRANCE

Although many of France's people live on farms and in small towns, the cities are part of what makes France so unique. Millions of people live in the capital of Paris, as well as other cities scattered throughout the country.

Paris

As well as being France's capital, Paris is also the country's largest city. Home to more than 2 million people, Paris is an important cultural, economic, and political center. The city is the seat of the national government and contains many famous landmarks and museums inside its borders.

The Eiffel Tower is the most visible landmark in Paris, towering 984 feet (300 meters) over the rest of the city. Built in 1889, this monument was built for the Universal Exhibition in celebration of the French Revolution. Between 1889 and 2017, more than 250 million people visited the Eiffel Tower.

Paris is also home to the Louvre, the famous art museum perhaps best known for its display of the

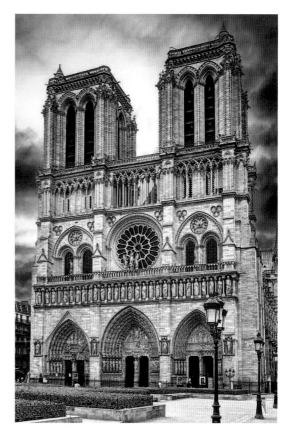

ABOVE: *Notre-Dame Cathedral, Paris.*

73

Educational Video

A sightseer's guide to Paris, the capital of France. The city attracts 42 million visitors a year.

ABOVE: *The Louvre art gallery was originally a seventeenth-century palace. The Pyramid was added in 1989. It was designed by Chinese-American architect, I. M. Pei.*

Mona Lisa. However, this is not all the museum has to offer. The Louvre has exhibits displaying art from **neolithic** times to the present.

Like most international centers of commerce and government, this city can be a little overwhelming at first. Cars rush by, seemingly bent on getting to where they need to go as fast as possible, all the while ignoring such trivialities as traffic lanes or stop signs. Then, once they reach their destination, it is not uncommon to see vehicles parked wherever there is room, even on the sidewalk.

Among all the bustle and glamour of the city, it is sometimes hard to remember the long history of Paris. The **catacombs** under the city provide a glimpse into what Paris used to be like. These huge caverns extend throughout the city, and some have lasted for more than 2,000 years. However, not all of this underground system is visible to the public. One can however go see, mass graves from the eighteenth century. It was at this time that the

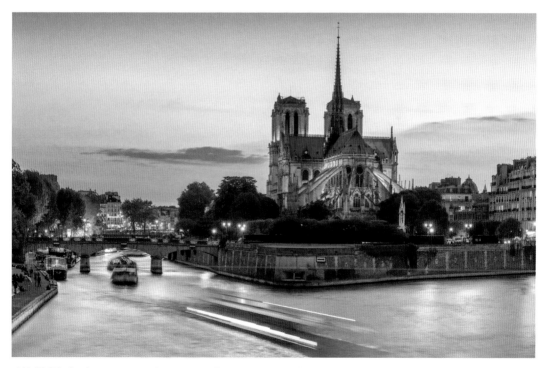

ABOVE: *A picturesque cityscape of Notre-Dame Cathedral in the Paris sunset.*

government of Paris realized their cemeteries were desperately overcrowded, and that the transportation of bodies to graveyards leftover from medieval times was a threat to the health of the people of Paris. So they converted some of the old underground tunnels into mass gravesites, even going so far as to carry millions of already buried bodies from the cemetery then in use to the new site.

Paris is a multifaceted city. On the surface is the rush of a city famous for its fashion and commerce. People hurry from place to place, never stopping to look up. On the other hand, Paris is a tourist attraction, full of varied monuments and museums, and impossible to fully enjoy no matter how long you spend there. And the action doesn't stop when darkness falls; Paris's nickname, the City of Lights, is well earned. Paris has something for everyone who visits, and no one will ever forget a visit there.

ABOVE: *The Saint Jean Castle and the Cathedral de la Major are situated near the Old Port of Marseille.*

Marseille

Marseille, on the Mediterranean coast, is the second-largest city in France. Founded in the sixth century BCE by Greek sailors, the city continues to be a home to diverse groups of ethnicities.

Marseille leads the health sector in France, home to a hospital complex that provides research and develops new equipment benefiting people all over the world. While it is a high-tech city, providing cutting-edge research, it is also a place that has been populated for more than 2,600 years, and as such is full of traditions and festivals.

The city is famous for its soap, as well as its production of *santons*—clay characters based on well-known figures of the area—that are put in Christmas

Château d'If, Marseille

The Château d'If is a fortress, and later a state prison, located on the island of If, the smallest island in the Frioul archipelago, situated offshore in the Bay of Marseille, in the Mediterranean Sea, southeastern France. It is famous for being one of the settings of Alexandre Dumas's adventure novel *The Count of Monte Cristo*, published in 1844.

crèches. The people of Marseille love to party and hold numerous celebrations throughout the year, including a **Candlemas** festival, where boat-shaped cookies called *navettes* are eaten, a kite-flying festival, and a garlic fair.

Because of its location on the Mediterranean Sea, Marseille is a popular tourist destination. People come from all over the world not only to enjoy the mild climate and take advantage of the many water sports available in the area but also to catch a glimpse of some of the breathtaking views around the city. Marseille also serves as a gateway: the rest of Provence is easy to travel to, making it an easy place around which to center one's trip.

Lyon

Lyon is an important manufacturing center, famous historically for its textiles and fabric production. Now, however, other industries have become more predominant, including chemical production, automobiles, and gasoline. Found where two major rivers, the Saône and the Rhône, meet, Lyon is the third-

ABOVE: *The Church of Saint Georges on the Saône River, Lyon.*

ABOVE: *The rooftops of Lyon with the Basilica of Notre-Dame de Fourvière in the background.*

largest city in France and boasts a population of just under 500,000. Because the city is located conveniently at the confluence of two major rivers, it has been a center of trade since its origins as a safe haven for the Celts.

While it is true that the textile industry, most notably the production of silk, has declined slightly in recent years, it still provides an important part of the culture of Lyon. Many well-known designers have their base in the city, which sports several museums about the history of this art and provides courses in design to anyone who is interested.

The home of Christianity in what was formerly Gaul, Lyon provided an important stepping-stone in the spread of this religion. Today, this is evident in the many ancient churches that stand throughout the city. However, though Christianity is an important part of Lyon's heritage, the city prides itself on its

ABOVE: The Cours Saleya is a large pedestrianized area, famous for its flower, vegetable, spice, and fish markets. It is one of the most popular places to visit in Nice.

religious tolerance; the city is home to many different religions, all able to coexist peacefully.

On December 8, the Feast of the Immaculate Conception, the city of Lyon lights up, with different colored lights on more than 200 of its important monuments, bridges, and buildings. This celebration stems from 1852, when the old bell tower on the ancient Basilica of Notre-Dame de Fourvière was restored. Because of rain on the night it was to be blessed, the bishop decided to cancel the light show that had been planned. Instead, the people of Lyon, without any planning at all, lit candles and lamps in their windows to celebrate this momentous occasion. Today, shopkeepers decorate the windows of their stores, and cruises allow visitors to see Lyon from the river.

Lyon is also a popular tourist destination, surrounded by beautiful mountains and near France's famous wine region. With its unique style and reputation in the fashion industry, it is no wonder that this city attracts people from all over.

Nice

Nice is mainly a resort city, as evidenced by its expensive hotels, restaurants of all kinds, and, of course, the casinos. While the new city is much like any other (either in France or anywhere else in the world), the old city is totally different—it's like stepping into another world. All of a sudden, the roads narrow and antique buildings crowd the streets, creating a very different feeling to the wide avenues, highways, and more modern architecture found in the rest of the city.

Perhaps Nice's most famous tradition is Carnival, a wild, ten-day celebration that signals the beginning of Lent. Begun in the Middle Ages, Carnival involves lots of parades, concerts, and food before people start fasting and setting their minds on the death of Jesus Christ. Each year, a king and a queen are crowned and are presented to their subjects in a parade with spectacular floats.

Like many other French cities, Nice contains traces of its past. Ancient Roman ruins can still be seen in parts of the town, showing that the past is never truly gone.

Text-Dependent Questions

1. When was the Eiffel Tower built?

2. What sea is Marseilles located next to?

3. How long does the Nice Carnival last?

Research Project

The city of Lyon is famous for its gastronomy. Write a report on the history of Lyonnaise cuisine.

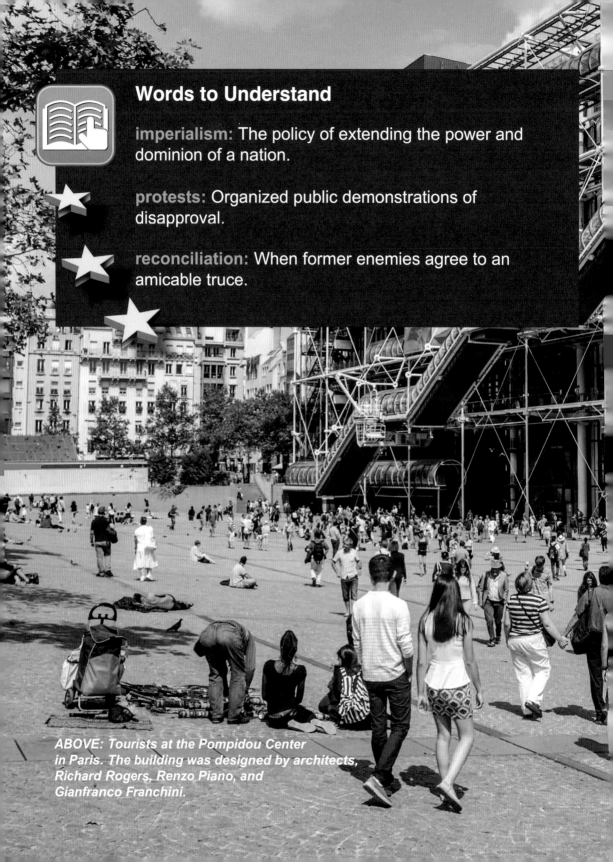

Words to Understand

imperialism: The policy of extending the power and dominion of a nation.

protests: Organized public demonstrations of disapproval.

reconciliation: When former enemies agree to an amicable truce.

ABOVE: Tourists at the Pompidou Center in Paris. The building was designed by architects, Richard Rogers, Renzo Piano, and Gianfranco Franchini.

Chapter Six
A BRIGHT FUTURE
FOR FRANCE

The European Union's Influence

A founding member of the EU, France has contributed much to the development of this new organization.

Since the end of imperialism and the dissolving of France's colonial holdings, the country has been in favor of an organization such as the EU—one that unites the various European countries. The reasons for this were varied, but included the fact that, without colonies, France was too small—as were most European nations—to have any international influence. Together, however, these countries could accomplish what was in all of their best interests.

France's Economy

The French economy is diversified across all sectors. The government has partially or fully privatized many large companies, including Air France, France Telecom, Renault, and Thales. However, the government maintains a strong presence in some sectors, particularly power, public transport, and defense. Despite terrorist attacks, labor strikes, and bad

ABOVE: French and EU flags.

ABOVE: *France has embraced the Euro unlike other countries such as Sweden and the UK who have kept their own currency.*

weather, France is still the most visited country in the world, with 83 million foreign tourists in 2016, including 530,000 who came for the 2016 Euro Cup. France's leaders remain committed to a form of capitalism in which they maintain social equity by means of laws, tax policies, and social spending that mitigate economic inequality.

Lower-than-expected growth and high spending have strained France's public finances. Despite measures to restore public finances after President François Hollande took office in 2012, France's public debt rose from 89.5 percent of GDP in 2012 to 96 percent in 2016.

President Hollande's policies aimed to enhance French industry's competitiveness and to lower high jobless figures. The Competitiveness and Employment Tax Credit of 2012, the Responsibility and Solidarity Pact of 2014, the Investment Stimulus Plan, and the Emergency Jobs Plan represent more than $42.6 billion in support for businesses in 2017 by lowering French labor costs, but so far the results of these policies have been marginal on France's competitiveness and job creation. In an effort to bolster social justice, the 2017 budget bill contained provisions to reduce income taxes for households and for small- and medium-sized enterprises.

During his mandate, President Hollande oversaw two highly unpopular economic reforms that led to widespread **protests**. The "Macron Law" of 2015, named after the current president, Emmanuel Macron, and enacted to boost economic growth, authorized businesses to open some Sundays each month and allowed flexibility to negotiate pay and working hours. The "El Khomri Law," imposed by decree in 2016, aimed to make it easier for businesses to employ people and gave employers more leeway to negotiate hours, wages, and time off.

ABOVE: *People outside the Louvre are gathered to celebrate the election of the new president of France, Emmanuel Macron, in May 2017.*

Renewable Energy in France

France has a target of producing 23 percent of its total energy needs from renewable energy by 2020 under its commitment to the renewable energy directive. This figure corresponds to renewable energy providing 33 percent of energy used in the heating and cooling sector, 27 percent of the electricity sector, and 10.5 percent of the transport sector's demand. By the end of 2014, renewable energy provided France with 14.3 percent of its total energy requirements, a rise from 9.6 percent in 2005.

Historically, the electricity sector in France has been dominated by the country's longstanding commitment to nuclear power. However, the publication of the 2016 Multi-annual Energy Program shows a commitment to rebalancing the electricity mix toward renewables. The report underlines the fact that by

ABOVE: The photovoltaic solar plant at Alès in southwest France. France has made a commitment to produce greener energy.

ABOVE: *France prides itself on its culture and takes good care of its ancient towns, historic sites, museums, and galleries. Petite France is one of Strasbourg's main attractions and is a UNESCO World Heritage Site.*

ABOVE: *In front of tens of thousands of people at the Carousel du Louvre, Emmanuel Macron gives his first speech, having just been elected president of France.*

2025 more than half of France's nuclear power capacity will come from stations that will be forty or more years old, and subject to either further work to extend their operation or closure. Renewable electricity capacity is planned to grow from 41 gigawatts (GW) in 2014 to between 71 and 78 GW by 2023.

Culture Budget

France has announced the largest cultural budget in the country's history amid falling museum attendance, which is linked to a drop in tourism resulting from 2015's terrorist attacks in Paris.

The French minister for culture and communication pledged to increase government funding for culture in 2017 by 6.6 percent, to €2.9 billion ($3.2 billion). He also announced that a cross-ministerial fund would set aside money to bolster the security infrastructure of French museums.

France Today and into the Future

Today, France is one of the most modern countries and a leader of Europe, having achieved a degree of **reconciliation** and cooperation with Germany that is central to the economic integration of Europe. It is instrumental in developing the EU's military capabilities and progress towards an EU foreign policy and trade.

France is playing an important part in the process of the United Kingdom leaving the EU (Brexit), and French politician Michel Barnier has been serving as the European Commission's chief negotiator for Brexit since December 2016.

In 2017 Emmanuel Macron was voted in as president of France. He is an ardent supporter of the European Union. Under Macron, France is set to ban the sale of any car that uses petrol or diesel fuel by 2040, in what the ecology minister has called a revolution.

Text-Dependent Questions

1. What companies have been privatized by the French government?

2. Is France committed to developing renewable energy?

3. Who is France's current president?

Research Project

Write a report about the state of the French economy today.

CHRONOLOGY

15,000 BCE	The first inhabitants settle in what is now France.
1 BCE	The Roman Empire attacks the region.
100 CE	Christianity begins to spread throughout France.
800	Pope Leo crowns Charlemagne head of the Roman Empire.
1152	Henry II, the king of England, and duke of Normandy, marries Eleanor of Aquitaine, making her the first woman to sit on the thrones of two countries: England and France.
1517	Martin Luther begins an attempt to reform the Catholic Church.
1789	Parisians attack the Bastille.
1789	The Declaration of the Rights of Man and of the Citizen is written.
1793	The, King Louis XVI, is tried and put to death.
1793	Maximillien Robespierre takes over the parliament and the Reign of Terror begins.
1814	Napoleon abdicates his throne and is exiled.
1815	Napoleon returns to France and is defeated at the Battle of Waterloo.
1914	France enters World War I.
1928	France joins the League of Nations.
1940	Hitler attacks France.
1944	Allied troops liberate France.
1982	President François Mitterrand attempts to nationalize most of the economy.
1991	France becomes a founding member of the EU.
1995	Jacques Chirac elected president
2002	The euro replaces replaces the French franc.
2007	Nicolas Sarkozy is elected President.
2008	France ratifies the Lisbon Treaty on reform of the EU.
2007	Françoise Hollande is elected president.
2015	Islamist gunmen shoot dead 17 people in Paris, most of them staff at magazine *Charlie Hebdo*.
2016	Islamist attacks in Paris and Nice.
2017	Emmanuel Macron is elected president.

Further Reading

Ardagh, John. Bailey, Rosemary. Fayard, Judith. Gerard-Sharp, Lisa. Jones, Colin. Kershaw, Alister. Lobrano, Alec. Roberts, Anthony. Tillier, Alan. Tisdall, Nigel. *DK Eyewitness Travel Guide: France*. London: DK, 2016.

McCormick, John. *Understanding the European Union: A Concise Introduction*. London: Palgrave Macmillan, 2017.

Mason, David S. *A Concise History of Modern Europe: Liberty, Equality, Solidarity*. London: Rowman & Littlefield, 2015.

Williams, Nicola. Averbuck, Alexis. Berry, Oliver. Carillet, Jean-Bernard. Christiani, Kerry. Clark, Gregor. Le Nevez, Catherine. Pitts, Christopher. Robinson, Daniel. *Lonely Planet France (Travel Guide)*. London: Lonely Planet Publications, 2017.

Internet Resources

France Travel Information and Travel Guide.
www.lonelyplanet.com/france

French Tourism.
http://us.france.fr/

France: Country Profile.
http://www.bbc.co.uk/news/world-europe-17298730

France: CIA World Factbook.
https://www.cia.gov/library/publications/the-world-factbook/geos/fr.html

The Official Website of the European Union.
europa.eu/index_en.htm

Publisher's note:
The website listed on this page were active at the time of publication. The publisher is not responsible for websites that have changed their addressees or discontinued operation since the date of publication. The publisher will review and update the website list upon each reprint.

INDEX

Picture Credits

All images in this book are in the public domain or have been supplied under license by © Shutterstock.com. The publisher credits the following images as follows:

Page 8: Petr Kovalenkov, page 12: EQRoy, page 13: IDN, page 23: thinpjang, page 42: Roman Yanusheusky, page 45: NeydtStock, page 54: CIS,page 58: Jan Kranendonk, page 60: Gumbo, page 66: ELEPHOTOS, page 67: Ferenc Szelepcsenyi, page 71: Ekaterina Pokrovsky, page 80: Rostislav Glinsky, page 81: Christian Mueller, page 85, 86: Frederic Legrand.

To the best knowledge of the publisher, all images not specifically credited are in the public domain. If any image has been inadvertently uncredited, please notify the publisher, so that credit can be given in future printings.

Video Credits

Page 12 Geography Now!: http://x-qr.net/1FeP, page 24 Rick Steves' Europe: http://x-qr.net/1DqM, page 49: Maria/city of Grasse: http://x-qr.net/1FeU, page 50: Viking River Cruises: http://x-qr.net/1Cvi , page 61: Datacube: http://x-qr.net/1FXh page 74: Expedia: http://x-qr.net/1D9d

Author

Dominic J. Ainsley is a freelance writer on history, geography, and the arts and the author of many books on travel. His passion for traveling dates from when he visited Europe at the age of ten with his parents. Today, Dominic travels the world for work and pleasure, documenting his experiences and encounters as he goes. He lives in the south of England in the United Kingdom with his wife and two children.